THE LAST YEARS OF
CARLISLE STEAM

A PICTORIAL JOURNEY

THE LAST YEARS OF
CARLISLE STEAM

A PICTORIAL JOURNEY

HOWARD ROUTLEDGE

Pen & Sword
TRANSPORT
AN IMPRINT OF PEN & SWORD BOOKS LTD.
YORKSHIRE - PHILADELPHIA

First published in Great Britain in 2021 by
Pen and Sword Transport
An imprint of
Pen & Sword Books Ltd.
Yorkshire - Philadelphia

Copyright © Howard Routledge, 2021

ISBN 978 1 52677 358 6

The right of Howard Routledge to be identified as author of this work has been asserted by him in accordance with the Copyright, Designs and Patents Act 1988.

A CIP catalogue record for this book is available from the British Library.

All rights reserved. No part of this book may be reproduced or transmitted in any form or by any means, electronic or mechanical including photocopying, recording or by any information storage and retrieval system, without permission from the Publisher in writing.

Typeset in 11/13 Palatino by SJmagic DESIGN SERVICES, India.

Printed and bound in India by Replika Press Pvt. Ltd.

Pen & Sword Books Ltd incorporates the Imprints of Pen & Sword Books Archaeology, Atlas, Aviation, Battleground, Discovery, Family History, History, Maritime, Military, Naval, Politics, Railways, Select, Transport, True Crime, Fiction, Frontline Books, Leo Cooper, Praetorian Press, Seaforth Publishing, Wharncliffe and White Owl.

For a complete list of Pen & Sword titles please contact

PEN & SWORD BOOKS LIMITED
47 Church Street, Barnsley, South Yorkshire, S70 2AS, England
E-mail: enquiries@pen-and-sword.co.uk
Website: www.pen-and-sword.co.uk

or

PEN AND SWORD BOOKS
1950 Lawrence Rd, Havertown, PA 19083, USA
E-mail: Uspen-and-sword@casematepublishers.com
Website: www.penandswordbooks.com

CONTENTS

Introduction		*6*
Acknowledgements		*7*
Chapter One	The Citadel	*9*
Chapter Two	Making Tracks Around Carlisle	*31*
Chapter Three	Carlisle District	*49*
Chapter Four	Kingmoor Motive Power Depot	*80*
Chapter Five	Upperby Motive Power Depot	*89*
Chapter Six	Canal Motive Power Depot	*96*
Chapter Seven	Signal Boxes	*102*
Chapter Eight	Demise in Colour	*107*
Chapter Nine	1T57	*114*
Bibliography		*116*

INTRODUCTION

The first railway company to arrive in Carlisle was the Newcastle and Carlisle Railway in 1836, and in the following forty years, another six railway companies also began operating into the border city.

The Midland was the last company to enter Carlisle in 1876 and with each of the seven companies eager to retain their independence, the railway infrastructure was therefore multiplied by seven, be it locomotive sheds, goods yards, goods depots, etc. During this period of expansion however, tracks were often realigned to accommodate the requirements of the incoming companies, although this was stabilised somewhat by 1877 with the completion of the network of goods lines running to the south and west of Citadel station. With such growth, Carlisle was becoming a major railway centre, albeit no doubt due to its geographical position more than anything else.

A major change to railway operations nationwide occurred with the 1923 Grouping, which saw all of the independent companies swallowed up with the creation of the 'Big Four', two of which took over railway matters in Carlisle: the London, Midland & Scottish (LMS) and the London & North Eastern Railway (LNER). This situation remained until 1948 when the railways were nationalised with the creation of British Railways (BR). Within seven years, however, in an effort to overcome competition from road transport, the 1955 Modernisation Plan was published which concluded that steam locomotives were to be phased out and replaced with diesel and electric traction, and vast marshalling yards using automated shunting were to be introduced in order to accelerate the movement of goods traffic.

As 1957 dawned, the steam locomotive was entering its final decade in Carlisle's rich and colourful history. Whilst certain parts of the country were to see steam completely eliminated from the early 1960s, Carlisle still retained a massive steam presence with its three locomotive sheds, but newly introduced diesel locomotives were now beginning to oust steam traction from some of the main line passenger workings, including all of the titled trains by 1963. The Modernisation Plan really swung into action during that same year, with the opening of a huge automated marshalling yard north of Kingmoor. This resulted in the closure of all of the smaller pre-grouping yards and all goods traffic was now being dealt with by locomotives from Kingmoor shed. 1963 was also the year that saw the closure of the former North British Canal shed with all of that depot's work also transferred to Kingmoor.

From the original seven pre-grouping locomotive sheds, Carlisle was now down to just two, Kingmoor and Upperby, but most of the goods traffic still remained steam-hauled and steam locomotives were still to be seen occupying the centre roads within Citadel station as they waited to relieve incoming passenger trains. That spectacle was diminished somewhat in September 1964, with the withdrawal from service of the last of the former LMS Pacifics, an occurrence that seemed to put a focus on the steady decline of the steam fleet, as other classes, formally employed on passenger duties, also began to be removed from the stock book. This gradual run down finally came to an end in Carlisle on 31 December 1967, with the closure of Kingmoor shed, some 131 years after the first locomotive had steamed into the city. Certain other parts of the north-west survived a further eight months until they also succumbed. By August 1968, it was all over; the steam locomotive powering the national rail network was consigned to the history books.

Living in Carlisle during the last years of steam had effectively blinded us from what was happening in other parts of the country as, even at the turn of the 1960s, Coronation class locomotives were still rolling into Citadel station at the head of express passenger trains, so in a way, we were rather blasé about it all ending in just a few years' time. Mindful that other areas had suffered a loss of steam by that juncture, I consider that I was fortunate to live in a part of the country that still allowed me to witness steam locomotive operations at such a busy railway centre where Stanier and Gresley Pacifics featured each day. Such observations eventually led on to photography, and with other like-minded enthusiasts living in the area, I attempted to record what was left of the steam era before it was too late. This group of enthusiasts is credited with a substantial number of the photographs contained in this book, captured whilst most of us were still teenagers armed with nothing more than a bicycle and a camera. In the main, cameras were primitive basic mechanical types, which were used in an attempt to emulate those photographs seen in railway magazines, but I don't think any of us were ever going to trouble the likes of W.J.V. Anderson and Bishop Treacy. What we had in our favour, though, was that we lived in Carlisle and were amongst its steam locomotives every day.

The book begins at a time when Citadel station was soon to be radically altered in 1957/58, and it endeavours to illustrate the final decade of steam activity in Carlisle and the surrounding area, bearing in mind that the Carlisle District, at one time or another, covered as far afield as Oxenholme, Beattock, Dumfries, and Workington. In addition to Carlisle, photographs are also included of the lines that radiated away from the city; particularly those severely graded ones that were such an attraction to steam photographers of the day.

Finally, although many hours have been spent dealing with the inevitable deterioration of a number of negatives now more than fifty years old, I have to admit that it has been an extremely rewarding experience and a most enjoyable trip down memory lane which featured a bygone age, the like of which will never be seen again.

Howard Routledge
Carlisle 2021

ACKNOWLEDGEMENTS

Without the help of the following people over a number of years, publication of the book would not have been possible, and I wish to acknowledge their kindness in allowing me the use of their photographs and transparencies.

Paul Irving, Ken Runton, Stephen Crook, Howard Milburn, Geoff Hamsher, Ken Armstrong, Geoff Routledge, Geoff Rixon, Derek Glover, Peter Brock, Jackie Brown, Howard Malham, David Goodfellow for the C. Blezard contribution, and Doug Gardner for the use of his father's photographs of Upperby Depot.

I am especially indebted to Martin Welch and Peter Fitton for their help and choice of photographs from their collections including the accompanying detailed notes.

A special mention is also due to Ian Cawthorne for producing the Carlisle Railway diagram, an absolute work of art.

8 • THE LAST YEARS OF CARLISLE STEAM

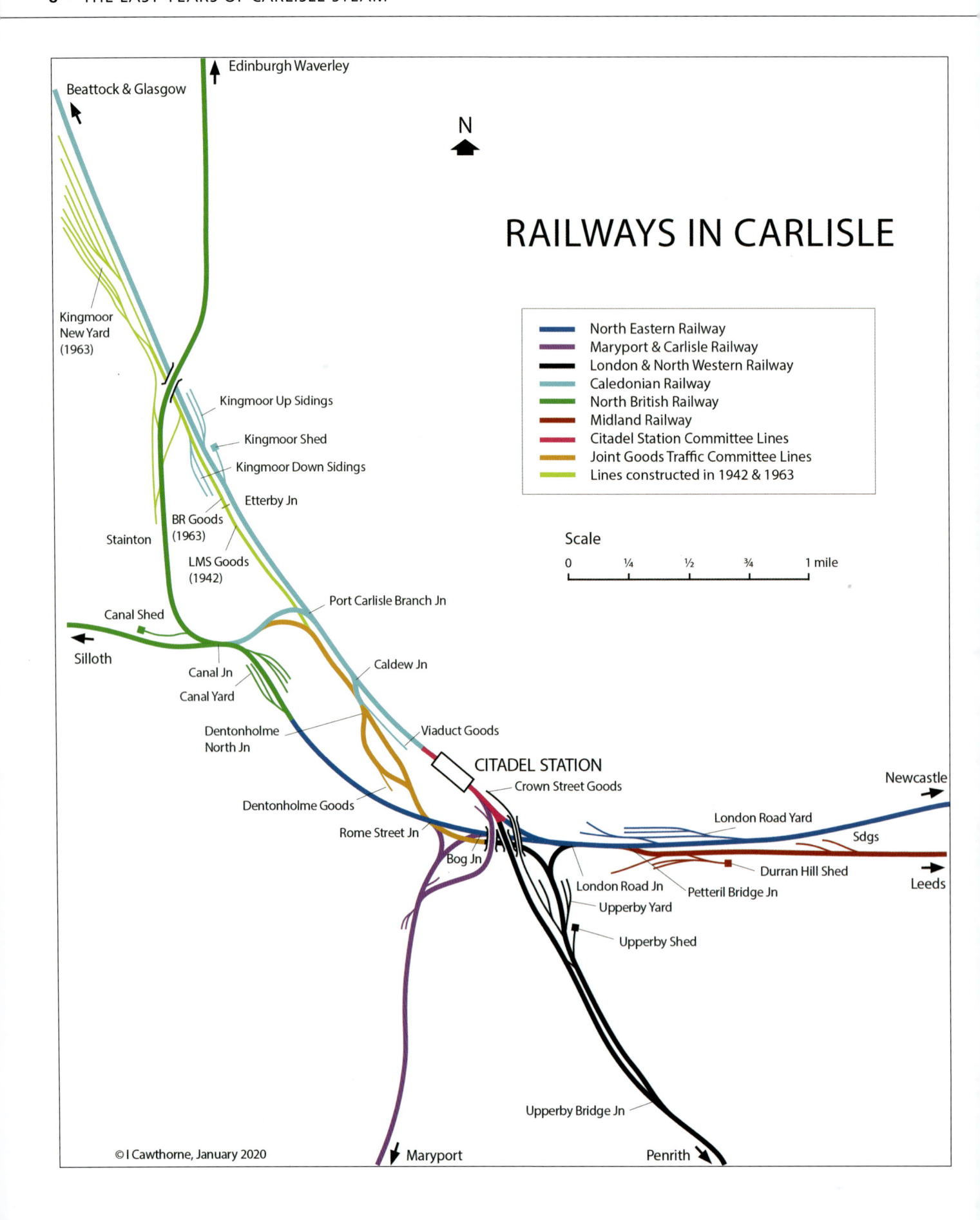

RAILWAYS IN CARLISLE

Legend:
- North Eastern Railway
- Maryport & Carlisle Railway
- London & North Western Railway
- Caledonian Railway
- North British Railway
- Midland Railway
- Citadel Station Committee Lines
- Joint Goods Traffic Committee Lines
- Lines constructed in 1942 & 1963

Scale: 0 – ¼ – ½ – ¾ – 1 mile

Locations labelled on the map:
- Edinburgh Waverley
- Beattock & Glasgow
- Kingmoor New Yard (1963)
- Kingmoor Up Sidings
- Kingmoor Shed
- Kingmoor Down Sidings
- Etterby Jn
- Stainton
- BR Goods (1963)
- LMS Goods (1942)
- Port Carlisle Branch Jn
- Canal Shed
- Silloth
- Canal Jn
- Canal Yard
- Caldew Jn
- Dentonholme North Jn
- Viaduct Goods
- CITADEL STATION
- Dentonholme Goods
- Crown Street Goods
- Rome Street Jn
- Bog Jn
- London Road Yard
- Sdgs
- London Road Jn
- Petteril Bridge Jn
- Durran Hill Shed
- Upperby Yard
- Upperby Shed
- Upperby Bridge Jn
- Maryport
- Penrith
- Newcastle
- Leeds

© I Cawthorne, January 2020

CHAPTER ONE
THE CITADEL

Fowler 2P 40651 acts as a pilot to Royal Scot Class 46145 *The Duke of Wellington's Regt. (West Riding)* as they depart Carlisle Citadel station with an up Thames-Clyde Express in August 1956. The original station opened to traffic in 1847 and was later to receive substantial alterations, completed in 1881, which included the fitting of full width Tudor style glazed end screens, as pictured. At the time this photograph was taken, the glass roof was becoming unsafe and the end screens were also in a poor state of repair which resulted in work commencing in 1957 to replace and drastically reduce the area of the covered roof. *A.J. Clarke/Colour Rail*

Stanier Princess Coronation Class 46229 *Duchess of Hamilton* makes a vigorous start from Citadel station with the up Royal Scot – first stop, London Euston. Compared to the previous photograph, this image shows to good effect how much of the station roof was removed during the 1957/58 renovation work. Also of note are the new platform canopies being erected as work progresses on the new end screen. *Paul Irving*

At first sight, it appears that the Caledonian express is awaiting departure from Carlisle to continue on its journey from Glasgow to London Euston; but it is apparent that the train pictured is actually northbound and is most probably not the Caledonian. The Caledonian train ran on weekdays only, but the train set was employed on a Saturday service between London and Glasgow, and that is what I believe is depicted here. This theory is supported by the lack of a tail lamp on the coach, as well as a loosely hanging hose, both clues that a locomotive change is taking place. It would appear that Camden based 46100 *Royal Scot* has brought the train north from Euston, and after being uncoupled, it is seen running light through the station towards Upperby shed. The Caledonian was usually allocated to a Coronation Pacific. *Paul Irving*

After arriving with the up Waverley express, Carlisle Canal A3 Class Pacific, 60093 *Coronach*, is pictured after being uncoupled from the stock prior to running light to the former North British shed. The amount of coal still within the tender is worthy of note after the locomotive's 100 mile run from Edinburgh, although its quality looks somewhat poor. *Paul Irving*

THE CITADEL • 11

The Royal Scot has arrived at Carlisle in 1959 behind Coronation Pacific 46231 *Duchess of Atholl* as 46247 *City of Liverpool* waits to take over for the 299-mile run to London Euston which was scheduled to be completed in five hours and eighteen minutes. Meanwhile, Kingmoor Black Five 45334 is in the process of coupling up to act as a pilot engine to the up Thames-Clyde Express. *Paul Irving*

Crewe North Stanier Black Five 44763 pilots Polmadie based Royal Scot Class 46107 *Argyll and Sutherland Highlander* as they depart Citadel station on 15 March 1958 with a heavy eighteen coach West Coast main line express. *Paul Irving*

12 • THE LAST YEARS OF CARLISLE STEAM

Proof that the sun didn't always shine on Carlisle, but the inclement weather certainly hasn't dampened the enthusiasm of a number of young enthusiasts as they take note of Camden's Coronation Pacific 46239 *City of Chester* after its arrival with the down Royal Scot.
Paul Irving

Another Canal A3 Pacific, this time 60095 *Flamingo*, has brought the Waverley into Citadel station and is drawing forward away from the stock whilst a double-headed combination, consisting of Stanier Class 6P 45613 *Kenya* and Black Five 45462, are prepared to work the train south over the former Midland main line. The rather slim-looking tender fitted to 45613 is one of the Fowler modified old standard high sided designs which had a reduced coal (7 tons) and water (3,500 gallons) capacity compared to the normal Stanier 4,000 gallon curved tenders which were attached to the majority of the class.
Paul Irving

THE CITADEL • 13

66A Polmadie allocated Royal Scot 46104 *Scottish Borderer* waits to relieve a down express in 1958. Built by the North British Locomotive Company, the engine completed 35 years' service prior to being withdrawn from Corkerhill shed in Glasgow at the end of 1962. *Paul Irving*

An unusually grubby Polmadie Pacific 46231 *Duchess of Atholl* appears ready for departure with the down Royal Scot whilst Canal shed Class J39 64932, and an unidentified Fowler 3F station pilot, occupy the centre road at the north end of Citadel station, circa 1958/59. *Paul Irving*

14 • THE LAST YEARS OF CARLISLE STEAM

The Royal Scot was the West Coast main line's premier express linking London Euston and Glasgow Central and was the preserve of the Princess Coronation class Pacifics, but it would appear that something has occurred to the booked locomotive as Crewe North based Royal Scot, 46118 *Royal Welch Fusilier*, has charge of the prestigious train as it enters Citadel station whilst running one hour late. The building to the left of picture is Crown Street Goods Depot, whilst No. 5 signal box stands opposite. *Paul Irving*

LMS built 2P 40687, pilot to Stanier Class 6P 45559 *British Columbia*, enters Citadel station with an up former Glasgow and South Western Railway (G&SWR) line express in 1959. Although the photograph has been captured in mono, it is apparent that the 2P's smokebox number plate and shed plate may have been painted a light blue, a custom that was employed at many Scottish based locomotive sheds. *Paul Irving*

THE CITADEL • 15

A classic scene at the south end of Citadel station shows 46241 *City of Edinburgh* ready for departure with train reporting number W126, the 1.30pm ex Glasgow-Euston Mid-day Scot; whilst 46257 *City of Salford* waits on 'B' road to relieve an incoming W484, the 10.20am ex Aberdeen -Euston express, circa 1959. *Paul Irving*

Fowler designed Patriot 45551 waits for departure with train reporting number W344, circa 1959. At this time, the locomotive was allocated to Carlisle Upperby and is pictured attached to a high sided 3,500 gallon tender which was once paired with Jubilee 45613 *Kenya*, as previously described. *Paul Irving*

Princess Coronation Class 46239 *City of Chester* stands at the head of the up Caledonian express on 8 September 1959. The Caledonian was a lightly loaded high speed train and was a late arrival to the West Coast scene, being introduced in 1957. *Ken Runton*

THE CITADEL • 17

After a locomotive change, 46226 *Duchess of Norfolk* departs with the 12.20pm ex Perth-Euston express. Originally streamlined, this locomotive spent most of its twenty-six years allocated to Carlisle and survived until 12 September 1964, a date when all of the remaining members (except 46256) of the class were withdrawn from service, en masse. *Paul Irving*

The Canal shed had four Gresley A3 Pacifics on its books and they would have rarely strayed away from the Waverley route or the odd excursion across to Newcastle. One of them, 60079 *Bayardo*, is pictured running through Citadel station on a date unknown but one that would have been near to the end of its career. The double chimney had been fitted during a visit to Doncaster Works in December 1959, but after only a couple of years' further service, the locomotive was withdrawn from traffic in September 1961. None of the Canal A3s were fitted with the German style smoke deflectors. *Kenneth Gray/Railscot*

18 • THE LAST YEARS OF CARLISLE STEAM

It would appear that both photographs have been taken at a time when the watering facilities at Canal shed have been out of order for some reason or another, as the two Peppercorn Haymarket Pacifics have been forced to take water at the station prior to working passenger trains over the Waverley route, circa 1959. The locomotives pictured, class A1 60152 *Holyrood* (top) and A2 60534 *Irish Elegance*, were regular visitors to Carlisle, as were the other former LNER Pacifics based at the Edinburgh shed. Their A4 locomotives, however, were more infrequent with their visits at that particular time. *Paul Irving (both)*

THE CITADEL • 19

Princess Royal
Class Pacific 46203 *Princess Margaret Rose* stands on A road waiting to relieve a northbound express during the summer of 1962 whilst it was allocated to Kingmoor and near to the end of its twenty-seven-year career with the LMS and British Railways.
Ken Armstrong

Victoria Viaduct
stands to the north of Citadel station as Princess Coronation 46256 *Sir William A. Stanier F.R.S.* re-starts the 1.35pm ex Euston to Perth express on 14 September 1963. It is believed that this was one of the last trains allocated to a Crewe North Coronation.
Martin Welch

20 • THE LAST YEARS OF CARLISLE STEAM

On 30 June 1963, the Railway Correspondence & Travel Society (RCTS) ran the Three Summits rail tour to include the climbs of Ais Gill, Beattock, and Shap. Commencing at Leeds, A4 Class 60023 *Golden Eagle* headed the train via Ais Gill to Carlisle where Coronation 46255 *City of Hereford* was waiting to relieve. The locomotive change is pictured (top) prior to 46255 taking the train onward for the climb of Beattock and onto Carstairs. Later that same day, a further locomotive change occurred at Carlisle involving A4 60004 *William Whitelaw*, which had brought the train down the former G&SWR line, and 60023, which took the final leg of the tour back to Leeds, via Shap, Low Gill, and Settle Junction. *Howard Milburn (top) P. Moffat/Colour Rail (bottom)*

THE CITADEL • 21

The road to Wembley! Well, Preston actually. On a bright 15 February 1964, a 5th round FA cup-tie against Preston North End saw three steam hauled special trains employed to convey Carlisle United supporters to the game in Lancashire. As with all of the football special trains at that time, Upperby shed turned out specially cleaned locomotives and, on this occasion, it included: rebuilt Patriots 45512 *Bunsen* on 1Z12, 45545 *Planet* on 1Z14, and Coronation 46238 *City of Carlisle* on 1Z13. *Author (both)*

Southern Merchant Navy Pacific 35012 *United States Lines* backs onto the stock of the RCTS Solway Ranger rail tour on 13 June 1964, prior to returning the train to Leeds via the former Midland main line. The tour had commenced at Leeds with the Southern Pacific hauling the train via Wennington to Carnforth then over Shap to Penrith. On arrival at Carlisle, the train was then taken to Silloth by two of the preserved Scottish veterans, the Caledonian Single 123, and Great North of Scotland (GNoS) 49 *Gordon Highlander*. *G.W. Routledge*

A photograph taken on 1 August 1964 shows to good effect the work carried out in 1957/58 which significantly reduced the area of the glass roof that previously had ran the full length of the high wall seen here at Citadel station. This area, on the west side of the station, was used predominantly for parcels traffic and some vans are pictured being marshalled by an Ivatt Class 4 locomotive, whilst Britannia Class Pacifics 70002 *Geoffrey Chaucer* and 70039 *Sir Christopher Wren* appear to be waiting to relieve incoming northbound trains. *D. Forsyth/ Colour Rail*

Another RCTS special train to include Carlisle and the northern hills in its itinerary was the Scottish Lowlander which ran on the 26 September 1964 and featured two Gresley A4s, and the last example of the Coronation class still in service. Starting at Crewe, 46256 *Sir William A. Stanier F.R.S.* hauled the train via Shap to Carlisle where 60007 *Sir Nigel Gresley* then took charge for an epic run over the Waverley route to Edinburgh. From there, 60009 *Union of South Africa* took the special train across to Glasgow, then down the former G&SWR line to Carlisle. The last leg, back to Crewe, featured 46256 again and once back on Crewe North shed, the locomotive was withdrawn from service, an event that brought an end to the Stanier Pacifics. 60007 is pictured (top) during the changeover at Carlisle as Royal Scot Class 46128 *The Lovat Scouts* stands in the background. The bottom image shows the final locomotive change after 60009 had arrived at Carlisle as light was failing, whilst 46256 waits to relieve prior to its final run. *Peter Fitton (top) H. Malham (bottom)*

Peppercorn designed Class A1 60154 *Bon Accord* of Neville Hill shed, Leeds, stands on A road during September 1964. Once again, parcel vans occupy A road sidings, whilst an unidentified Britannia class locomotive stands ahead of them.
G.W. Routledge

Presumably, Edinburgh St Margaret's A3 60041 *Salmon Trout* has brought an express over the Waverley route into Citadel station on 3 July 1965 as Kingmoor Black Five 45135, and a Britannia Pacific, wait to relieve southbound workings. Unfortunately, the 1M55 train reporting number board prevents positive identification of the Britannia, but the photographer's notes indicate that in all probability, the locomotive was 70031 *Byron*.
Howard Milburn

On 11 December 1965, the Warwickshire Railway Society promoted the Waverley rail tour using no fewer than five steam locomotives throughout the day's events. Starting at Birmingham, the special train travelled to Leeds from where former LMS class 5XP 45697 *Achilles* took charge for the run over the Settle to Carlisle line (S&C). Arrival at Carlisle (left) was met with wet and dismal weather prior to Dundee based A2 60528 *Tudor Minstrel* taking the next leg of the tour over the Waverley route to Edinburgh. *Author (both)*

26 • THE LAST YEARS OF CARLISLE STEAM

Kingmoor Black Five 44692 was built at Horwich Works during 1950 which classified it as being one of the younger members of the 842-strong class of locomotives; it is pictured leaving Carlisle on 30 April 1966 with a down express. Irrespective of the locomotive's age, however, it was reported as being withdrawn from service within fourteen days of this picture being taken. *Author*

Leeds Holbeck Class 6P 45593 *Kolhapur* runs towards 5 bay platform on 30 April 1966 with 1X50, a special train conveying Huddersfield Town football supporters to a league fixture against Carlisle United. Of note is the Stanier 3,500 gallon tender rather than the more common 4,000 gallon type. Known by enthusiasts as Jubilees, the class, when introduced by the LMS in 1934, were officially identified as 5XP, later changed to 6P5F and in 1955 they were re-classified to 6P. To avoid any confusion, I will refer to the class from this point on as Jubilees. *Author*

THE CITADEL • 27

A picture full of contrast features a grimy Kingmoor Britannia Pacific 70033 which is now devoid of its *Charles Dickens* nameplates. The fireman, no doubt, will be completing the coupling-up procedure before adding a second lamp onto the buffer beam to show an express lamp code. *Geoff Hamsher*

28 • THE LAST YEARS OF CARLISLE STEAM

A member of the footplate crew of 70001 *Lord Hurcomb* has purloined the train reporting number board 1X28 from the incoming locomotive and he is now affixing it to his Britannia Class engine prior to departure with a down express on 27 May 1966. *Author*

By mid-1966, the steam scene at Carlisle was in its last eighteen months and the variety and colour that once adorned proceedings within Citadel station was certainly a thing of the past as the regular steam hauled passenger workings were now featuring just a handful of different classes of locomotive. During this gradual run-down, the sight of any green or black paint certainly wasn't an option, a situation that is adequately displayed in this scene by the grime covering 70036 *Boadicea* (nearest) and 70054 *Dornoch Firth* on 27 May 1966. *Author*

THE CITADEL • 29

Unique Black Five 44767, the only member of the class fitted with Stephenson link motion, double-heads with 70004 *William Shakespeare* hauling the Locomotive Club of Great Britain (LCGB) Fellsman rail tour which is pictured arriving at Carlisle on a very wet 4 June 1966. *Geoff Hamsher*

More Britannia action as 70029 *Shooting Star* departs Citadel station with an up 1X10 special working in July 1966. Formally allocated to Cardiff Canton shed, the locomotive was transferred to Carlisle in 1964, serving at both Upperby and Kingmoor before being withdrawn from traffic near to the end of steam in October 1967. *Author*

The South & West Railway Society ran the Granite City rail tour over two days beginning on 3 September 1966 from Euston to Aberdeen via the West Coast main line to Carlisle then over the Waverley route to Edinburgh. This is the scene at Citadel station during a locomotive change involving Britannia 70032 *Tennyson*, which had bought the train from Preston, and one of the last surviving members of the V2 Class, 60836, which had been specially supplied by Dundee Tay Bridge shed to work the train on to Edinburgh. *Author*

With only three months left of steam traction at Carlisle, special trains continued to appear to offer enthusiasts their last steam hauled experience over the northern fells. One such tour, which ran on the 30 September 1967, had been arranged by the A4 Locomotive Society and titled 'The Splendour of Steam Rail Tour', which featured two privately owned locomotives. Commencing at Peterborough, former Great Western Castle Class 7029 *Clun Castle* hauled the train via the S&C and is pictured entering Citadel station, whilst A4 4498 *Sir Nigel Gresley* waits to return the train south. *Author*

CHAPTER TWO
MAKING TRACKS AROUND CARLISLE

Britannia 70045 *Lord Rowallan* is pictured entering Carlisle at its southernmost point on the West Coast main line whilst running tender first with a loaded train of limestone from Hardendale Quarry at Shap, to Kingmoor New Yard in June 1966. At the nearby Upperby Bridge Junction, the train will divert onto the former London & North Western Railway (LNWR) goods lines that will allow it to bypass Citadel station. *Author*

Former North British Class J36, 65321, is seen at Upperby Yard whilst employed on Trip No. 46 duties on 9 June 1962. A number of locomotives from the Carlisle sheds were employed transferring wagons between the former pre-grouping yards, a ritual that ceased in 1963 with the opening of the New Yard at Kingmoor. Upperby shed's antiquated coaling tower stands to the right of the picture. *G.M. Staddon/Transport Library*

Same location as the previous photograph but looking across towards Upperby locomotive shed as Liverpool Edge Hill Black Five 45242 passes on the up goods line during the mid-1960s. Although Upperby yard will have ceased to function to marshal goods traffic by that time, it was still in use for wagon and carriage storage. *Geoff Hamsher*

A short distance further north, and Royal Scot 46115 *Scots Guardsman* passes under St. Nicholas Bridge on the up goods line heading towards Upperby to then gain access to the West Coast main line at Upperby Bridge Junction. *S.C. Crook*

MAKING TRACKS AROUND CARLISLE • 33

Kingmoor Black Five 44673 pilots Jubilee Class 45619 *Nigeria* as they pass London Road Junction with an up Waverley express in 1959. The photographer was a fireman at Kingmoor, and he had arranged for his colleagues to produce this dramatic smoke effect even though a 20mph speed restriction was only 300 yards ahead at Petteril Bridge Junction. *Peter Brock*

Blackpool Central Jubilee, 45705 *Seahorse*, is pictured with an up goods train whilst passing under the West Coast main line as it progresses towards Upperby. The set of lines seen beyond the locomotive are the former NER lines from London Road Junction. *S.C. Crook/ Armstrong Railway Photographic Trust (ARPT)*

34 • THE LAST YEARS OF CARLISLE STEAM

After passing under three closely spaced bridges that included the West Coast main line, Standard Class 9F 92208 passes Bog Junction signal box on 20 July 1966 with a down goods train conveying what appear to be military vehicles. The 9F is travelling on the former NER lines from London Road Junction whilst the former LNWR tracks are seen on the right. From this point at Bog Junction, those former LNWR lines were extended in 1877 to form the Carlisle Joint Goods lines. *D. Forsyth/Colour Rail*

Work-stained Britannia 70035 *Rudyard Kipling* passes Bog Junction on the former Joint Goods line whilst heading towards Upperby in June 1966. The lines seen branching off left ran towards Maryport. *Author*

MAKING TRACKS AROUND CARLISLE • 35

There was a good mixture of pre-grouping locomotives allocated to the Canal and Reid designed N15 69155 is a classic example; classified 3MT, the 0-6-2 tank was built by the North British in 1910. Running south on the former Joint Goods, the locomotive is working Trip No. 48 as it passes Denton Holme Goods Station on 19 September 1959. *G.M. Staddon/ Transport Treasury*

Black Five 45120 passes Denton Holme North Junction signal box with a down goods on 13 April 1965. The tracks branching to the right led into Denton Holme Goods Yard from the opposite end as pictured above, whilst the derelict land opposite the box, where the Ford Anglia is parked, was previously the Caledonian's Viaduct Yard. *D. Forsyth/Colour Rail*

36 • THE LAST YEARS OF CARLISLE STEAM

A photograph taken from Denton Holme North Junction signal box in December 1965 highlights Stourton allocated Stanier Class 8F 48130 as it heads towards Kingmoor New Yard with a down goods. There has probably been an issue with the Joint Goods line that day, as all goods traffic had been diverted to run through Denton Holme Goods Yard. *Author*

MAKING TRACKS AROUND CARLISLE • 37

Land once occupied by the Caledonian Railway Viaduct Yard is slowly returning to nature whilst its former goods sheds stand empty awaiting demolition as Leeds Holbeck Jubilee 45697 *Achilles* heads north away from Citadel station with a Birmingham-Glasgow express on 10 July 1965. *Howard Milburn*

The Ford Anglia car makes its second appearance which gives the impression that it may have been owned by one of the signalmen working in Denton Holme North Junction box as Kingmoor Black Five 45135 emerges from under Caldew Bridge with an up goods on 12 November 1966. *Howard Milburn*

The Solway Ranger was an RCTS rail tour which ran on the 13 June 1964 and commenced at Leeds with a Southern Merchant Navy Class locomotive in charge. From Carlisle, the train was entrusted to two preserved veterans; ex Great North of Scotland Railway 4-4-0, 49 *Gordon Highlander,* and ex Caledonian Railway Single 123, for the journey to Silloth and return. After what appears to be a spirited departure from Carlisle, both regulators have been eased to allow the locomotives to coast along to Port Carlisle Branch Junction where they will turn off the West Coast main line to head towards Canal Junction to gain access to the branch line to Silloth. *Peter Fitton*

Stanier Black Five 45480 passes Port Carlisle Branch Junction with a down parcels train during August 1965. Due to the refurbishment of the bridge that carried the main passenger lines over the River Eden, south of Kingmoor, the locomotive is crossing to the down goods line in order to bypass the closure. *Author*

MAKING TRACKS AROUND CARLISLE • 39

This is Port Carlisle Branch Junction; the photograph is undated but probably taken around 1960 and shows Coronation Pacific 46243 *City of Lancaster* getting into its stride with a down express. The lines seen on the extreme right are the Carlisle Joint Goods lines and they ended a short distance further onto the branch. The goods lines continuing north from this point were a late addition to the Carlisle scene, being laid in 1942 and continued to run parallel to the West Coast main line, and from 1963, they connected with the New Yard at Kingmoor. *S.C. Crook*

Gresley A3 Class Pacific 60090 *Grand Parade* leaves the West Coast main line and gains access to the Port Carlisle Branch line, and after a short distance it will reach Canal Junction from where the locomotive will run onto the Waverley route for its journey to Edinburgh. *S.C. Crook/ARPT*

A view from the fireman's seat of an unidentified Jubilee as it heads north on the down goods towards Kingmoor whilst passing Coronation Class 46229 *Duchess of Hamilton*. The image has been recorded pre-May 1960 which was the time when the fireman/photographer transferred from Kingmoor to the Canal shed in order to work on A3 class locomotives over the Waverley route. *Peter Brock*

A fortuitous shaft of evening sunlight illuminates Britannia Class 70036 *Boadicea* as it crosses the River Eden at the head of 1S93, a Saturday relief to the Mid-day Scot, on 31 July 1965. *Author*

Stanier Jubilee
45660 *Rooke* was built at Derby in 1934 and in 1937 it took part in a number of dynamometer car test trains on the S&C and G&SWR lines with a view to the acceleration of services on those routes. It certainly appears to be a world away from those heady days as the locomotive is pictured after leaving Kingmoor shed in May 1966; *Rooke* was withdrawn from service at Holbeck within the following four weeks. *Author*

42 • THE LAST YEARS OF CARLISLE STEAM

Only five years separate the two photographs and the changes around Etterby Junction are quite apparent. The top photograph was taken in July 1961 and shows the former Caledonian Railway down yard and Etterby Junction signal box, both of which were swept away with the opening of the New Yard in 1963. The bottom image was recorded on 2 July 1966 and shows a busy scene with at least three steam locomotives and a diesel waiting for a break in main line traffic before they can exit Kingmoor shed. The Waverley route can be seen crossing the West Coast main line in the far distance, whilst the lighting towers of the New Yard are beyond.
R. Horton/Colour Rail (top) Author (bottom)

MAKING TRACKS AROUND CARLISLE • 43

Etterby Junction was always a busy section of railway especially with the movements of locomotives coming off Kingmoor shed before heading north to the New Yard; a move which is what we see here. Standard Class 5 73154, the last steam locomotive to be built at Derby Works, was allocated to 66B Motherwell in this September 1966-dated photograph. *Author*

The cycle ride to Kingmoor has been somewhat cold in the freezing conditions that prevailed throughout a dark December day in 1965 where we see an unidentified Britannia Class Pacific at Etterby Junction after leaving the 12A shed. The train reporting number plate, which inconveniently obscures the locomotive's identity, is an indication that the engine is heading towards Citadel station to relieve 1M87. *Author*

Liverpool Edge
Hill Black Five 45094 heads north towards Kingmoor marshalling yard on a Saturday evening, 31 July 1965. As a result of the closure of the former Caledonian down yard, this area became popular with local steam photographers. *Author*

Withdrawn by British Railways in 1963, A3 Pacific 4472 *Flying Scotsman* was purchased by Alan Pegler, who began to use the locomotive to haul special charter trains, one of which, organised by the Gainsborough Model Railway Society, is seen passing Kingmoor as it heads north to Dumfries on 15 May 1965. *Author*

MAKING TRACKS AROUND CARLISLE • 45

Kingmoor allocated 45105 passes its home depot with an up empty stock working on 31 July 1965. The building seen beyond the turntable was the engineman's hostel which is now a privately owned block of apartments. *Author*

44086 was a Midland designed class 4F locomotive built by Kerr, Stuart at Stoke and entered service in 1925. It is pictured heading past Kingmoor shed with a goods train from west Cumberland in August 1965. *Author*

An enthusiast's special train that headed direct to Kingmoor shed was the Pennine Tour which was run by the Warwickshire Railway Society on 4 September 1965 featuring the preserved A3 Class Pacific 4472 *Flying Scotsman*. The A3 is pictured ready for departure from Kingmoor as a filthy Bank Hall allocated Jubilee 45721 *Impregnable* speeds past with the 2pm ex Glasgow to Liverpool express. *Author*

By spring of 1966, only thirteen Jubilee Class locomotives were still in service, the majority of them being allocated to sheds at Holbeck, Farnley, and Wakefield. The Holbeck ones were regular visitors to Carlisle at that time, working both goods and passenger trains into the city; one of them, 45697 *Achilles*, is seen running tender first towards Kingmoor New Yard in April 1966. *Author*

MAKING TRACKS AROUND CARLISLE • 47

Stanier Black Five 44738, fitted with Caprotti valve gear, runs tender first towards the New Yard on 4 September 1963; the 6G shed code indicates that the locomotive is from Llandudno Junction. Speaking to a number of former drivers at Kingmoor, they were quite scathing of Caprotti locomotives, claiming that they were poor hill performers, something not recommended on many of the lines that radiated away from Carlisle. *Peter Fitton*

An unidentified Stanier 8F is pictured en route to Kingmoor New Yard whilst closely following a preceding goods train. The goods lines in Carlisle were worked by a permissive block system which meant that more than one train could be allowed into a single section at any one time; obviously, this called for the upmost diligence by footplate staff. *Geoff Hamsher*

48 • THE LAST YEARS OF CARLISLE STEAM

Kingmoor power signal box (PSB) stood at the entrance to the New Yard and in the shadow of the bridge carrying the Waverley route over the West Coast main line. Holbeck Black Five 44852 runs tender first to Kingmoor shed after depositing its goods train in the reception sidings in August 1965. *Author*

There is still newness about Kingmoor New Yard in this August 1965 picture of pioneer Ivatt Class 4 43000 heading south away from the up departure roads. The yard, thought at one time to be the largest in Europe, covered an area of 480 acres with 72 miles of track, and had the capacity to handle 5,000 wagons per day. *Author*

CHAPTER THREE
CARLISLE DISTRICT

THE LANCASTER & CARLISLE RAILWAY

The fireman appears to have just completed a round of firing on Black Five 44727 as it climbs the 1 in 131 grade past Brisco with an up goods train in September 1966. The locomotive, which was allocated to Kingmoor throughout its eighteen-year service, was withdrawn near to the end of steam during October 1967. *Author*

Britannia Class Pacific 70045, minus its *Lord Rowallan* nameplates, climbs past Brisco cutting, some four miles south of Carlisle, with an up goods on 9 July 1966. It was during that year that the locomotive acquired oval buffers, the only member of the class to do so. *Author*

50 • THE LAST YEARS OF CARLISLE STEAM

The 5A shed plate denotes that Black Five 44683 is a Crewe North engine that has been rostered by Upperby shed to work 1M54, a Newcastle to Blackpool express, which is pictured near Wreay on 9 July 1966. Today's M6 motorway passes underneath the West Coast main line at this location. *Author*

Crewe North Black Five 44763 passes Penrith No. 1 signal box with an up goods in December 1964. The fireman has obviously been busy in his preparation for the climb to Shap Summit, some thirteen miles distant. *G.W. Routledge*

CARLISLE DISTRICT • 51

To accommodate the building of the M6 Motorway, railway bridges had to be installed at various points to carry the West Coast main line above the course of the new road. In these two fascinating photographs, we see preparation work underway for a bridge to be placed into position south of Penrith. The work took place between the 2 and 5 June 1967. The larger of the two decks was to take the double track main line whilst the single line deck was for the down main line loop which also accommodated bi-directional traffic for the Cockermouth, Keswick & Penrith branch (CK&P). An unidentified Britannia Pacific hurries northbound (top) on Friday 2 June prior to the West Coast main line being severed, which is pictured (bottom) on the following day. Once the tracks had been lifted, the two decks could then be slid into position, a procedure witnessed by quite a large crowd. *Martin Welch (both)*

52 • THE LAST YEARS OF CARLISLE STEAM

After a gentle three mile climb from Penrith, the grade then stiffens to 1 in 125 for the next seven miles where we see Polmadie Royal Scot 46121 *Highland Light Infantry, City of Glasgow Regiment* at Thrimby with a Glasgow to Manchester Victoria express on 4 August 1962. *Peter Fitton*

A short distance further south and Carnforth Black Five 45212 approaches Thrimby signal box during an all-out attack towards the summit with a 1M32 Glasgow to Morecambe train on 31 July 1965. *Peter Fitton*

CARLISLE DISTRICT • 53

One of the lesser known titled trains, the Lakes Express ran during the summer months to serve a number of holiday destinations in the north-west of England. Coronation Pacific 46250 *City of Lichfield* is pictured at Shap Summit with the down Lakes Express on 31 August 1963. The train, which originated at Euston, would have already dropped off a number of coaches at Oxenholme in order for them to be worked on to Windermere, whilst the remaining coaches continued north to Penrith for onward transmission to Keswick, then Workington. From Penrith, the train would normally be hauled by an Ivatt class 2 2-6-0, whilst 46250 would then run light engine to its home depot at Upperby. The choice of locomotive for the Lakes Express could vary amongst several classes, but the heavier Saturday train was usually rostered for a Coronation Pacific. *Martin Welch*

A most unusual sight at Shap Summit as preserved Caledonian Single, 123, heads north, most probably back to its home shed at Dawsholm, Glasgow. Research as to what the locomotive could have been doing so far south revealed one explanation in that it had hauled a charter train from London Victoria to the Bluebell Railway on 15 September 1963. *J.A. Brown*

54 • THE LAST YEARS OF CARLISLE STEAM

The climb from Carlisle to Shap Summit is over allowing the fireman to relax on Britannia 70051 *Firth of Forth* as it speeds downgrade through Shap Summit Cutting with 1M31, an Aberdeen to Manchester express, on 31 August 1963. *Martin Welch*

Shap bank with its 1 in 75 gradient was a severe obstacle to steam hauled traffic heading north on the West Coast main line and banking engines were stationed at Oxenholme and Tebay to help those heavy trains that required assistance. Pictured within the final mile of the climb, Stanier Class 8F 48439 of Royston shed passes Shap Wells with a lengthy p-way train on 6 November 1965. Rear end assistance is being provided by one of Tebay's banking engines, Fairburn 2-6-4T 42232. *Peter Fitton*

CARLISLE DISTRICT • 55

The cold air on a winter's day accentuates the exhaust from Patricroft Class 8F 48491 as the locomotive tackles the climb whilst passing Shap Wells on 20 December 1967. Whether the driver decided to go it alone, or if no banking engine was available at this late stage of steam activity at Tebay shed, we will never know. However, within the following two weeks, scenes like this were consigned to the history books, as steam traction in Carlisle District had finished. *Peter Fitton*

The daily ritual at Tebay is captured from the station footbridge as one of the 2-6-4T locomotives stationed at the nearby shed begins to assist a down goods train up to the summit on 14 May 1964. The lines seen branching off to the right led to Kirkby Stephen East and Stainmore. *Martin Welch*

A few minutes later and Kingmoor Black Five 44689 runs downgrade with an up goods train. The station, which was built by the Lancaster and Carlisle Railway company, opened in 1852 and was closed from 1 July 1968 – then demolished to make way for a more modern and sterile railway scene. *Martin Welch*

CARLISLE DISTRICT • 57

For those trains needing a helping hand on both Grayrigg and Shap banks, the assisting locomotive would be attached to the front at Oxenholme, a procedure which is illustrated here as Fowler 2-6-4T 42414 and Jubilee Class 45598 *Basutoland* speed through Tebay with a Blackpool Central to Glasgow relief on 15 August 1964. *Peter Fitton*

58 • THE LAST YEARS OF CARLISLE STEAM

A Black Five hauled goods stands at the foot of Shap bank on 13 September 1966 awaiting Fairburn 2-6-4T 42154 to exit Tebay shed to bank the train up to the summit. From Tebay, the initial gradient is 1 in 146 for approximately one mile from where it then tightens to 1 in 75 for the next four miles up to the summit. *Author*

The Fowler 2-6-4T locomotives which had been the mainstay at Tebay for many years were replaced by Stanier and Fairburn types, and in the final few months of steam traction on the northern fells, a number of Standard 4-6-0 tender engines were also transferred there for banking duties. One of the new arrivals, 75039, is pictured leaving the shed environs to assist a down goods up to the summit on 26 August 1967. *Martin Welch*

CARLISLE DISTRICT • 59

Another view from the footbridge, this time looking south, highlights Tebay locomotive shed which at this time was coded 12E and it was certainly out of keeping with the rest of the railway buildings there, having being built as late as 1950. A Fairburn 2-6-4T stands by ready for the call to duty on 25 August 1966. *Martin Welch*

Tebay station on 13 September 1966, and Britannia Class Pacific 70018 *Flying Dutchman* of Upperby shed hurtles south with a parcels train. Although the Stainmore line was closed from 1962, the former interchange yard is still in use at this time going by the number of wagons seen situated there. *Author*

Another train being assisted from Oxenholme features Stanier 2-6-4T 42665 and Black Five 44905 as they pass through Tebay in readiness for the final assault up to Shap Summit on 13 September 1966. *Author*

Dillicar water troughs were situated in the Lune Gorge, south of Tebay, where we see 45376 replenishing its tender tank whilst hauling an up ballast train on 27 August 1964. The 'X' sign gave an indication to the fireman exactly where the trough commenced, although this would have been more of assistance to him during the hours of darkness, more than anything else. *Martin Welch*

CARLISLE DISTRICT • 61

The fireman on Coronation Pacific 46237 *City of Bristol* has lowered the tender scoop to allow the locomotive to replenish its tank as it passes over Dillicar water troughs whilst heading a down fast fitted goods on 14 May 1964. *Martin Welch*

Kingmoor Standard 72008, *Clan Macleod,* appears well prepared for the climbs ahead as it passes Oxenholme shed with an afternoon combined Manchester/Liverpool to Glasgow express on 29 August 1964. The four road shed, which had opened in 1880 to provide banking engines to assist heavy trains up to Grayrigg Summit, was included into Carlisle District in 1960 with the shed code 12G; closure came during July 1962. *Martin Welch*

THE MIDLAND RAILWAY

The Durran Hill area was occupied by two of the pre-grouping companies, the Midland and the NER. The signal box pictured is controlling former NER rails and it more or less identifies the dividing line that existed between the two companies as they ran parallel to each other on the approach into Carlisle; Midland on the left, NER to the right. Stanier Black Five 45028 heads an up 1N85 passenger working as it leaves Carlisle on 7 August 1965; pictured bottom left, is the site of the Midland Railway's Durran Hill locomotive shed, after demolition. *D. Forsyth/Colour Rail*

A photograph that has been taken from above Culgaith Tunnel shows Standard Class 9F 92058 with the down empties from Widnes to Long Meg on 3 June 1967. Culgaith was one of only two locations on the line to warrant a level crossing, the gates of which appear to have been opened to road traffic quickly after the passage of the train. The signalman will have had quite a busy shift that day as the S&C was being used as a diversionary route for West Coast main line traffic due to an engineer's possession near Penrith. *Martin Welch*

A short distance south of Appleby station was the Express Dairy that displayed a sign proudly boasting 'Milk for London'. Ivatt Class 4MT 43045 is busy shunting the milk tanker wagons into position there on 29 July 1965 prior to hauling loaded tanks to Carlisle from where they will be shipped to London via the West Coast main line. *Martin Welch*

BR Standard Class 9F 92075 appears to be making heavy weather on the 1 in 100 grade whilst passing through Kirkby Stephen station with a train of hopper wagons loaded with anhydrite from the Long Meg mine to Widnes on 30 July 1966. No doubt the fireman will be looking for some respite from his labours once the summit at Ais Gill, some seven miles distant, is reached. *Martin Welch*

64 • THE LAST YEARS OF CARLISLE STEAM

Hauling a load that will not tax the capabilities of a Black Five locomotive too much, 44767 is pictured heading towards Birkett Tunnel with a southbound pick-up goods on 1 April 1967. *Peter Fitton*

Ais Gill Viaduct stands towards the head of the Mallerstang Valley where Carlisle Kingmoor Stanier Class Five 44902 is pictured on the final part of the climb to the summit with an up goods on 30 April 1966. *Martin Welch*

CARLISLE DISTRICT • 65

High summer it may be, but the weather conditions seen here, rain, coupled with low cloud, is such a common feature on the upper reaches of the S&C that one can be forgiven for holding the impression that the area appears to have its own weather pattern completely divorced from other parts of the country. Climbing the final few yards up to the summit amidst such inclement weather conditions, Stanier Jubilee 45626 *Seychelles* has charge of the 9.50am Edinburgh to Leeds SO express on 31 July 1965. *Peter Fitton*

Britannia 70014 *Iron Duke* crests the summit at Ais Gill on 30 July 1966 with 1M27, a SO summer relief to the up Thames-Clyde Express. The fifteen-mile climb from Ormside, mainly at 1 in 100, is now complete as the locomotive passes the summit board denoting it is 1,169' above sea level. *Martin Welch*

A strong westerly wind soon whips the locomotive's exhaust across the desolate moorland as Standard Class 9F 92075, previously pictured struggling at Kirkby Stephen, finally reaches the summit at Ais Gill. The photographer has had ample time to record both images as the seven-mile climb from Kirkby Stephen to the summit has taken the 9F no less than forty minutes. *Martin Welch*

A photograph taken from the short length of track that led to the turntable at Garsdale shows the signal box from where the 1910 Hawes Junction Disaster was played out when signalman Sutton, who was under immense pressure whilst dealing with no fewer than nine pilot engines that had arrived from Ais Gill for turning, forgot about two of them which were sitting on the down main line; a lapse that was to result in a collision with the 'Midnight Express' that claimed the lives of twelve passengers. Matters at Garsdale seem a bit more peaceful on 16 July 1961 as Hughes Class 5MT 42793 passes with a down goods. *Peter Fitton*

Jubilee Class 45593 *Kolhapur* passes Blea Moor loops on 26 August 1967 with a down relief to the Thames-Clyde Express. Time was certainly running out for the three survivors of the class still allocated to Leeds Holbeck shed as the depot was closed to steam locomotives just two months later. *Martin Welch*

After taking water in the down loop at Blea Moor on 19 August 1967, Stanier Class 8Fs 48077 and 48506 restart a concrete sleeper track panels train en route from Castleton P-way Dept. to Carlisle. *Martin Welch*

THE CALEDONIAN RAILWAY

A peaceful scene at Quintinshill, one mile north of Gretna, that will be briefly disturbed by the passage of Kingmoor's Royal Scot 46115 *Scots Guardsman* as it approaches with the 9.25am Crewe to Perth express on 28 November 1964. Once the train had passed, and the signals returned, the peace and tranquillity of such a rural location would prevail once more. It is difficult to comprehend that this exact location was the scene of Britain's worst railway disaster which occurred on 22 April 1915 involving three trains, one of which was a troop train conveying soldiers of the 1/7th Battalion of the Royal Scots from Larbert to Liverpool in order to embark for Gallipoli. The death toll was 226, with a further 246 injured. *Kenneth Gray/RailScot*

The Caledonian Railway's Carlisle to Glasgow line opened in 1848 and it included the fearsome ten mile climb north from Beattock station, a gradient which averages between 1 in 69 to 1 in 88. Although banking engines were stationed at Beattock, Stanier Black Five 45437 is making an unassisted run at the bank with what appears to be a lightweight Carlisle to Perth parcels train on 25 May 1967. *Martin Welch*

CARLISLE DISTRICT • 69

The two new paraffin lamps are in complete contrast to the external condition of Dumfries allocated Black Five 44995 as it draws a goods train out of the loops at Beattock for the climb up to the summit on 3 June 1966. The volcanic exhaust seen down by the shed indicates that a banking engine is already providing assistance and when it comes into view (bottom) it is identified as Fairburn 2-6-4T 42693. Beattock locomotive shed had been within the Carlisle District with the code 68D until 1962 when it then moved into Glasgow District to become 66F. *Martin Welch*

Fairburn Class 4 banking engines, 42129 and 42169, are doing their upmost to raise the roof as they depart Beattock on 4 June 1965 as they make an all-out effort to push a diesel hauled goods up to the summit. *Martin Welch*

Harthope was a popular location with steam photographers and it is easy to see why, as Stanier Class Five 45082, assisted by one of Beattock shed's banking engines, is pictured climbing hard with a heavy Ravenscraig bound limestone train on 10 June 1965. *Martin Welch*

THE NORTH BRITISH RAILWAY

The North British line between Edinburgh and Carlisle, the Waverley route, opened in 1862 and was closed as a result of the Beeching Report on 6 January 1969. The company did not actually reach Citadel station but ran as far south as Canal Junction, from where it had obtained running rights on Caledonian rails via Port Carlisle Branch Junction to the station. Black Five 45293 is pictured with a solitary brake van in tow passing Stainton as it heads towards Canal Junction in August 1965. This was most probably one of the final runs for the locomotive in BR service as it was reported as being withdrawn from traffic that same month. *Author*

Stainton level crossing was within one mile of Canal Junction and it had an archaic system of operation which certainly belonged to a bygone age. There was a crossing keeper's cottage situated there and the crossing gates were always open to road traffic during the daytime. Beside the cottage there was a small box on a wooden post which contained a bell and an indicator. When a train was due, the bell rang and the indicator moved, which was the signal for the woman there to appear from the cottage to close the gates. Stanier Class 8F 48223 is heading north towards the New Yard at Kingmoor in April 1966; this part of the Waverley route was used by goods traffic that avoided Citadel station by using the former NER line from Rome Street Junction. *Author*

72 • THE LAST YEARS OF CARLISLE STEAM

Gresley Class V2 60835 gets away from Stainton with a goods train, most probably the 2.15pm to Millerhill. In order to access the Waverley route, the V2 will have drawn its train tender first from the New Yard to the Stainton loop via the chord line seen in the foreground. From there, it will have then run round its train prior to setting off for Millerhill, as pictured. The loop line is seen in the previous photograph, immediately ahead of the 8F. *S.C. Crook/ARPT*

An unusual sight of a Heaton A1 Pacific on the Waverley line in April 1962, as 60132 *Marmion* heads north away from Riddings Junction. The local passenger train lamp code displayed indicates that the locomotive is most probably restarting its train away from the nearby station. The viaduct seen in the background carried the Langholm branch line across the Liddel Water. *S.C. Crook/ARPT*

CARLISLE DISTRICT • 73

The branch line from Riddings Junction to Langholm was seven miles in length and for many years was worked by one of the Canal's J39 class, as seen here with 64964 at Broomholm in May 1959. After the demise of the J39s, the service was handled by either an Ivatt class 4MT 2-6-0, or one of the 2-6-4Ts recently allocated to the Carlisle shed. *S.C. Crook*

St Margaret's B1 61244 *Strang Steel* leaves Riccarton Junction with the 2.15pm Carlisle to Millerhill goods in August 1964. Climbing at 1 in 75, the locomotive still has two miles to go before reaching the summit at Whitrope. Riccarton was the junction of the Waverley Route and the Border Counties Line from Hexham; the latter closed to traffic in 1958. *S.C. Crook/ARPT*

The Carlisle to Silloth branch line came under the control of the North British in 1862, then the LNER, and ultimately British Railways, before it was axed in 1964 as a result of the Beeching cuts. With it being only twenty-three miles distant, the seaside town was popular with Carlisle residents and the line was well patronised in the pre-car era, especially at weekends. Here we see what must be a heavier train than normal requiring a double-headed J39 combination of 64733 and 64888 passing the Canal locomotive shed. *E.E. Smith/Transport Library*

A further look at the RCTS Solway Ranger charter train as it arrives at Silloth station on 13 June 1964, three months before the closure of the line. The lead locomotive, Great North of Scotland 49 *Gordon Highlander*, was built in 1920 and was withdrawn from service in 1957. The Caledonian Single 123, however, was of 1886 vintage and it lasted until 1935. British Railways decided to restore both locomotives in 1957/58 for hauling special trains and this most welcome situation lasted until 1966 when the pair were finally retired and placed into the Glasgow Museum of Transport. *Peter Fitton*

GLASGOW & SOUTH WESTERN RAILWAY

The Glasgow & South Western Railway line from Glasgow to Gretna Junction via Kilmarnock and Dumfries was opened in 1850. To access Carlisle however, the company had running powers over Caledonian rails for the nine miles from Gretna Junction. Standard Class 76073 runs through Annan station with a down pick-up goods train on 12 June 1965. *Martin Welch*

Britannia 70036 *Boadicea* passes a rather desolate Dumfries shed on 11 June 1965 with a coach that is being removed from an up passenger train; one can only assume that a defect on the coach had caused such action to be taken. Dumfries shed came within the Carlisle District for many years having the shed codes 12G and 68B until 1962 when it then became 67E in a district headed by Glasgow Corkerhill. *Martin Welch*

76 • THE LAST YEARS OF CARLISLE STEAM

Kingmoor Stanier
Black Five 44883 is turned at Dumfries on 10 June 1965. Although the locomotive is connected to the table's vacuum pipe, the turning procedure looks as though it is being assisted with a physical contribution. *Martin Welch*

Kingmoor's last Caledonian built locomotive had been placed into store in July 1961 but an active allocation of such locomotives was still to be found after that time at Dumfries. Built at the Caledonian Railway's St Rollox Works in 1887, Drummond 2F 'Standard Goods' 57302 is pictured at Dumfries shed; the 68B shed plate is a clue that the photograph was taken no later than 1962. Withdrawal came in October 1963 after a career spanning seventy-six years. *Ken Armstrong*

CARLISLE DISTRICT • 77

A busy scene at Dumfries on 11 June 1965 as Standard Class 76073 leaves with the 8.20am to Stranraer, whilst Britannia 70009 *Alfred the Great* stands ready for departure with 3S03, a Carlisle to Glasgow parcels train. It is believed that the three mail coaches seen behind the locomotive would have been worked on to Ayr from Kilmarnock. *Martin Welch*

Black Five 45365 makes a rather smoky departure from Dumfries on 10 June 1965 with a down goods train. The tracks in the foreground of the picture branching off the main line were to Stranraer. *Martin Welch*

MARYPORT & CARLISLE RAILWAY

Of all of the main lines that radiated away from Carlisle, the Maryport and Carlisle was the only one where locomotive crews were not faced with a severe gradient at some point on the route. Ivatt 43025 heads west at Cummersdale on the outskirts of Carlisle; the 12F shed plate indicates that the photograph was taken some time between 1960 and 1963 prior to Workington shed acquiring the code 12D. *S.C. Crook*

Kingmoor Black Five 44899 heads a Barrow to Carlisle goods through Aspatria. Although undated, the photograph will have been after 1963, a period when top lamp-irons were moved to a lower position on the smokebox door, an action designed to prevent footplate crews from being electrocuted whilst changing lamp codes when underneath overhead electrified wires. *Paul Irving*

NORTH EASTERN RAILWAY

Two photographs taken by signalman Ken Runton on 4 March 1958 from Durran Hill (NER) signal box shows Canal B1 Class 61395 (top) with the 12.20pm ex Newcastle to Carlisle express. Built at the North British Locomotive Works in Glasgow, the locomotive entered service during 1952 and was allocated to the Carlisle shed from then until June 1962 when it was transferred to Gorton. The bottom image shows K1 Class 62010 of Blaydon shed approaching the box with a down goods. *Ken Runton (both)*

CHAPTER FOUR
KINGMOOR MOTIVE POWER DEPOT

An impressive line-up at Kingmoor in June 1962 includes Princess Royal Class 46201 *Princess Elizabeth*, Hughes Class 5MT 42882, and an unidentified Princess Coronation. 1962 was the last year for the Princess Royals and the three remaining ones at Kingmoor, 46200, 46201, and 46203, were withdrawn from service by November of that year. The Hughes mogul class had been associated with the shed for many years and no fewer than twenty-five examples were allocated there at the turn of 1960; they too suffered massive withdrawals in 1962. *Kenneth Gray/RailScot*

It appears that Jubilee 45657 *Tyrwhitt* hasn't required turning as it has skirted around the turntable to exit Kingmoor whilst passing A3 Pacific 60052 *Prince Palatine* which is at the head of a queue to use the 70ft table on the 4 September 1963. *Peter Fitton*

KINGMOOR MOTIVE POWER DEPOT • 81

During April 1961, a number of Coronation Pacifics were transferred from Upperby to Kingmoor and two of them, 46244 *King George VI* and 46255 *City of Hereford,* stand ready for their next turn of duty in 1963. A Stanier Class 8F and a Fowler 2-6-4T, seen in the background, complete the scene. *M. Chapman/Colour Rail*

A total of thirty Standard Class 5 locomotives were fitted with Caprotti valve gear and a number of them were regular visitors to Carlisle whilst allocated to depots in the Glasgow area. One such locomotive, 73153, is seen running down towards the turntable on 4 September 1963. *Peter Fitton*

On the Sunday morning of 17 May 1964, I visited Kingmoor shed and this was the scene that greeted me - Coronation Pacifics 46257 *City of Salford*, 46244 *King George VI*, and BR Standard 72008 *Clan Macleod*, lined up as if a slide rule had been used. I stood directly ahead of the locomotives and viewed the scene through my camera, but having only a couple of exposures left on the roll of film, I decided not to take the shot and looked for something more interesting! Some years later I mentioned this occurrence to Howard Milburn who, I then discovered, had followed me round Kingmoor later that same day and bagged the photograph we see here. *Howard Milburn*

The external condition of Kingmoor's Jubilee, 45613 *Kenya,* is typical of the standard that prevailed towards the end of steam, but it certainly isn't an indication as to the mechanical condition of the locomotives in use at that time. The Jubilee has obviously just received attention to its fire causing a safety valve to lift but its departure from the shed isn't due for some time yet because of its position at the rear of the depot. *Geoff Hamsher*

Stanier Princess Coronation Pacific 46225 *Duchess of Gloucester* is pictured passing the breakdown crane shed at Kingmoor, circa 1964. This locomotive took part in a number of controlled road tests on the S&C in 1956 whilst hauling simulated loads up to 900 tons; in addition, it then underwent further testing on the rollers at the Rugby Test Plant. Whether by design or otherwise, the full results of those tests were never published, unlike reports concerning other locomotives that took part in identical testing at that time. *Geoff Hamsher*

In December 1963, fifteen Britannia class locomotives were transferred to Carlisle from the Eastern Region. Nine, including 70009 *Alfred the Great*, were moved from March shed to Kingmoor, whilst Immingham depot transferred its six to Upperby. I recall visiting both Kingmoor and Upperby sheds on a Sunday morning in early December 1963 and it certainly involved some surprises. 70009 is in a reasonably clean condition as if recently ex-works, whilst pictured at Kingmoor in the mid-1960s. *Geoff Hamsher*

84 • THE LAST YEARS OF CARLISLE STEAM

Kingmoor had a small allocation of Fowler 2-6-4Ts until about 1963 so it is somewhat of a puzzle as to why this Leeds Holbeck Class 4 tank 42394 was on shed during April 1965. *Geoff Hamsher*

The fireman of a Dalry Road B1, 61307, takes a break from preparing the locomotive to pose for the photograph at Kingmoor during April 1965. The train reporting number 6S61 referred to an Edinburgh goods working that was routed via Carstairs on the West Coast main line. The Edinburgh based driver of the locomotive is seen walking away from the scene after a 'technical discussion' with a Kingmoor inspector about the merits, or otherwise, of the B1 class. *G.W. Routledge*

KINGMOOR MOTIVE POWER DEPOT • 85

Another ex LNER interloper, this time in the form of V2 60931, has arrived on shed after working a goods train from Edinburgh in April 1965. After having been coaled, it has taken its place on the ash pit awaiting disposal. *G.W. Routledge*

St Margaret's V2 Class, 60813, appears fully prepared to leave the depot during April 1965. This locomotive was a unique member of the class in that it had a stovepipe chimney and small smoke deflectors fitted. *G.W. Routledge*

Another set of Edinburgh footplatemen pose for the camera before leaving the shed in April 1965 with former LNER A3 Pacific 60052 *Prince Palatine*. After the closure of the Canal shed, Edinburgh based locomotives became daily visitors to the former Caledonian depot. The final three members of the class still in service at this time, 60041, 60052, and 60100, were all allocated to St Margaret's shed and were regularly employed hauling goods traffic over the Waverley route. 60052 went on to be the last survivor of the class, being officially withdrawn in January 1966. *G.W. Routledge*

Carnforth's Stanier Class 8F 48519 lays a smoke screen across Kingmoor whilst being prepared for its next duty in April 1965. The locomotive appears to be in quite a clean external condition as if recently out of works; the larger than normal numerals seen on the cabside were usually associated with a visit to Darlington Works. *G.W. Routledge*

KINGMOOR MOTIVE POWER DEPOT • 87

After hauling the 1.35pm goods from Millerhill to Carlisle, B1 Class 61350 of St Margaret's shed has run down to Etterby Junction before reversing onto Kingmoor depot on a sunlit Saturday evening, 31 July 1965. *Author*

After the demise of the more venerable classes of locomotives based at Hawick, a number of Standard types were allocated there from the early 1960s that included two 2-6-4 tanks which featured quite regularly on local stopping trains to Carlisle. One of them, 80113, is pictured ready to leave Kingmoor depot in August 1965 to work the 6.13pm local to Hawick. *Author*

88 • THE LAST YEARS OF CARLISLE STEAM

The derelict land opposite Kingmoor shed was an excellent location for steam photography and was popular with a number of like-minded friends at that time. Motherwell Black Five 44820 has been turned and is already in back gear awaiting the signal to depart the shed and cross over the main lines before running on the down goods line to the New Yard in August 1965. *Author*

Former Great Western Castle Class 7029 *Clun Castle* causes a lot of interest as it makes a rare appearance at Kingmoor on 14 October 1967 whilst being turned prior to running down to Citadel station to head the return working of 1T80, an LCGB Castle to Carlisle tour. *Geoff Hamsher*

CHAPTER FIVE
UPPERBY MOTIVE POWER DEPOT

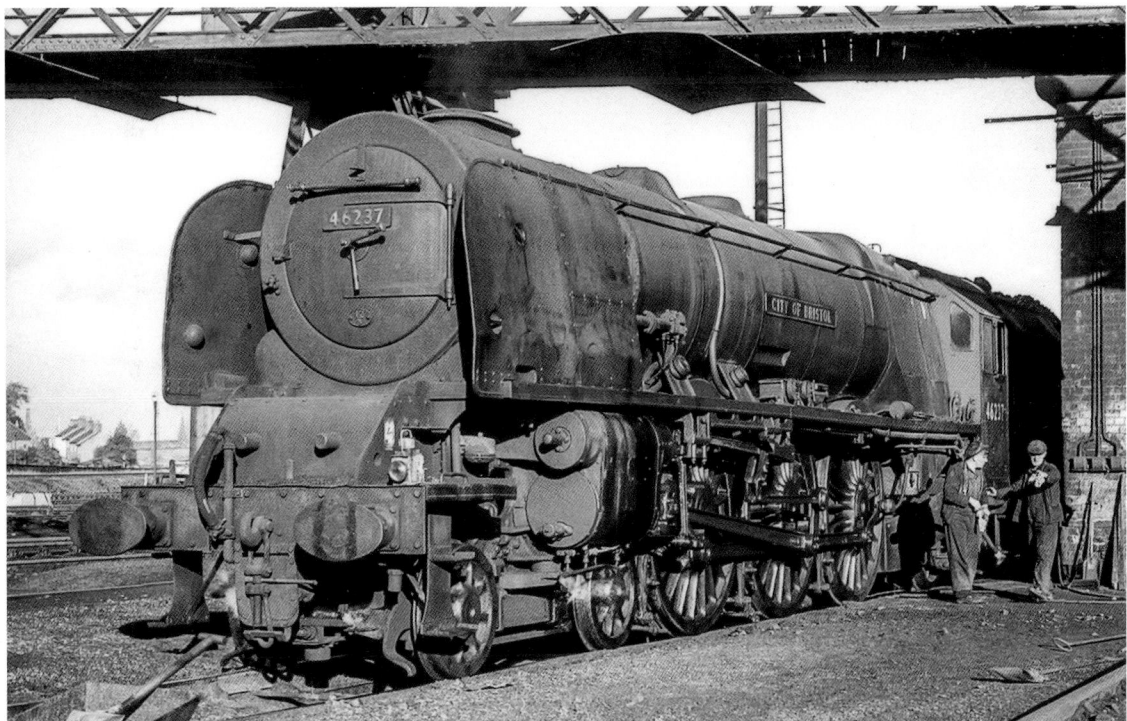

Two images recorded by Upperby driver David Gardner show Coronation class Pacifics 46238 *City of Carlisle* and 46237 *City of Bristol* occupying the ash pit on the shed's arrival road during the early 1960s. It is somewhat puzzling that both locomotives are facing south and have well stocked tenders; one would expect such locomotives to have been north facing and coupled with near empty tenders whilst occupying that part of the shed. The original depot at Upperby was built by the Lancaster and Carlisle Railway and underwent many changes before the LMS commenced construction of the familiar concrete roundhouse which was completed in 1948. *David Gardner*

90 • THE LAST YEARS OF CARLISLE STEAM

Undated, but the photograph will most probably have been taken during the 1963 Big Freeze and shows a triple-headed snow plough unit consisting of Fowler 4F 44346 and two unidentified Black Five locomotives awaiting their next call to duty. The severe freezing conditions, which covered the whole country, started in late December 1962 and lasted through to March the following year. *Derek Glover*

Upperby had a small number of Ivatt Class 2 2-6-0 locomotives on its books and they were employed on a variety of tasks including local trip workings, pilot duties at Citadel and Crown Street Goods, in addition to Keswick line services. 46455 is pictured backing down towards the roundhouse where Coronation Pacific 46250 *City of Lichfield* stands on 4 September 1963. *Peter Fitton*

UPPERBY MOTIVE POWER DEPOT • 91

A low afternoon sun highlights those huge 6ft 9in diameter driving wheels of Stanier Coronation 46238 *City of Carlisle* as it stands outside the roundhouse of its home shed on 17 November 1963. *Howard Milburn*

A view looking north towards Upperby shed and yard on 7 March 1964 features 46225 *Duchess of Gloucester*. The lattice footbridge seen in the background, which crossed over the West Coast main line and Upperby Yard, was the preferred way into the shed by many local to the area. *Kenneth Gray/RailScot*

Crewe North
Coronation Pacific 46251 *City of Nottingham* fills the 70ft turntable within the roundhouse during July 1964. This really was the final year for the roundhouse hosting a shed full of ex LMS passenger locomotives, and it was certainly much poorer for the loss of its fleet of Stanier Pacifics, an event that occurred within eight weeks of this photograph being taken. *Howard Milburn*

With Carlisle's entire fleet of Coronation Pacifics now permanently withdrawn from traffic, 46256 *Sir William A. Stanier F.R.S.* is the last one to appear at Upperby in steam as it is prepared to haul the final leg of the Scottish Lowlander rail tour to Crewe on 26 September 1964. The locomotive had been given a reprieve from the mass cull of the class, carried out earlier that month, due to an agreement already in place between BR and the RCTS for it to haul the tour. *Howard Malham*

UPPERBY MOTIVE POWER DEPOT • 93

Stockport Edgeley
Jubilee 45654 *Hood* stands on the arrival road at Upperby in January 1965. The photograph was taken from the footbridge previously mentioned that ran from opposite Hasell Street, and, most conveniently, dropped you right beside an entrance into the roundhouse. *Author*

Together with 70004, Britannia 70014 *Iron Duke* was allocated to Stewarts Lane depot during 1953-1958 to work the Southern Region's prestigious express, the Golden Arrow; the bolts seen towards the bottom of the locomotive's smoke deflector is an indication where the large arrow symbol was once fitted. It is a far cry from such duties as 70014 is pictured on one of the roads emanating from the roundhouse at Upperby on 19 April 1965. *David Gardner*

94 • THE LAST YEARS OF CARLISLE STEAM

Both Kingmoor and Upperby had Fowler 4F Class 0-6-0s on their allocations but by the time this photograph was taken in August 1965, all of them had either been withdrawn from traffic or transferred away. Although other members of the class were on Upperby shed that day, 44086 was the only one in steam having worked in with a goods train from west Cumberland the previous day. *Author*

Britannia Pacific 70030 *William Wordsworth* was transferred from Crewe South shed to Upperby in early August 1965, which is when this photograph was taken. It would appear that the locomotive has been in need of some maintenance work upon arrival at the Carlisle shed. *Author*

UPPERBY MOTIVE POWER DEPOT • 95

Carnforth Black Five, 45374, stands in a deserted yard at Upperby in August 1965. Such a desolate scene as this can most probably be put down to two reasons: the opening of the New Yard at Kingmoor – once that occurred all goods traffic was lost to Kingmoor shed; and the loss of a number of steam-hauled passenger workings on the West Coast main line. *Author*

A commendably clean Ivatt 2MT 2-6-2T 41222 is pictured on the arrival road at Upperby awaiting disposal on 30 January 1966; the lamp code indicates that the locomotive had most probably been employed on station pilot duties. Once again, another empty scene at a once bustling steam shed and goods yard. It will come as little surprise to learn that Upperby closed to steam on 12 December that same year. *Author*

CHAPTER SIX
CANAL MOTIVE POWER DEPOT

Out of a class of 184 locomotives, only eight of the Gresley V2s were bestowed with names, one of which, 60835 *The Green Howard, Alexandra, Princess of Wales's Own Yorkshire Regiment,* is pictured going onto the turntable at the Canal shed on 29 June 1958. *Martin Welch*

With a single lamp code displayed, albeit on the wrong iron, Newcastle Heaton V2 60945 appears ready for departure from the Canal shed on 29 June 1958. Continuing with the Gresley theme, the Canal's very own Class D49/1 62734 *Cumberland* stands alongside. *Martin Welch*

CANAL MOTIVE POWER DEPOT • 97

The photograph has been taken from the coal elevator and provides a birds-eye view of the turntable which is occupied by St Margaret's K3 61988. The roadway seen in the picture ran from Newtown Road and had the rather apt name of Engine Lonning which allowed road vehicle access to the shed. The single line track beyond is the branch line to Silloth. *Fleetwood Shawe/ ARPT*

The classic lines of a Gresley A3 Class Pacific are all too apparent as 60035 *Windsor Lad* stands outside the Canal shed waiting on its next call to Waverley line duty. The locomotive was a Haymarket engine for most of its twenty-seven years' service, but it was transferred to the Canal in May 1961 for a brief three month period before being returned to the Edinburgh shed from where it was withdrawn from service in September that same year. *Ken Armstrong*

Built by the North British Locomotive Company at their Cowlairs Works in 1897, J36 Class 65293 rests between duties outside the wheel drop shed which was situated at the rear of the Canal depot. The locomotive was a long-term resident at the Carlisle shed and was withdrawn from traffic near to the end of 1962, which was the year that saw the demise of the remaining pre-grouping locomotives still allocated to the former North British shed. *Derek Glover*

With a number of pre-grouping North British and Gresley locomotive classes coming to the end of their working life, former LMS types began appearing at the shed including a number of the 2-6-4T variety. One such locomotive, Stanier Class 4 42440, is pictured on the roundhouse turntable on 14 July 1962. The stalls within the roundhouse were quite short in length, which ruled out their use by most of the shed's allocation of tender engines. *D. Forsyth/Colour Rail*

CANAL MOTIVE POWER DEPOT • 99

Moving into the final days of the Canal shed on 26 May 1963, and no fewer than eight different classes of locomotives are on display with centre stage being held by an A4 Pacific, 60012 *Commonwealth of Australia*. Once again, the photograph has been taken from the coal elevator and it gives an informative view of the shed layout including the absence of a roof to the straight road shed seen on the extreme right. *A.R. Thompson/ARPT*

June 1963 and closure is now only a matter of days away, but we still have a classic Canal shed scene and apart from the WD 2-8-0 seen to the left of picture, the remainder are all Edinburgh St Margaret locomotives, including an A3, two V2s, A2/3 60522 *Straight Deal*, and A3 60041 *Salmon Trout*. S.C. Crook/ARPT

Saturday 8 June 1963, the penultimate weekend before closure, and the two former LNER Pacifics in the previous picture (top) are still on shed; 60522 *Straight Deal*, and 60041 *Salmon Trout*, but now joined by another A3 Class locomotive, 60043 *Brown Jack*. Howard Milburn

CANAL MOTIVE POWER DEPOT • 101

The following day, Sunday 9 June 1963, and A3 60043 *Brown Jack* has moved to the front of the shed building with V2 60825 alongside. The majority of the A3 Class locomotives were named after racehorse Classic winners and *Brown Jack*, which was the last A3 to be built (1935), was named after the 1929 to 1934 winner of the Queen Alexandra Stakes. *Howard Milburn*

The final photograph of the Canal shed, taken on Sunday 9 June 1963, features (L to R): 45100, 43000, 60522 *Straight Deal*, 60041 *Salmon Trout*, 45102, 44986, 60129 *Guy Mannering* (from Tweedmouth shed) and B1 class locomotives. The shed, which had been built by the North British Railway Company after their arrival into the border city in 1862, had lasted more than 100 years before being deemed surplus to requirements. After 15 June 1963 the shed was abandoned and all of the depot's work was transferred to Kingmoor. *Howard Milburn*

CHAPTER SEVEN
SIGNAL BOXES

Ken Runton was a British Railways signalman who worked in many of the signal boxes around Carlisle. He was also a competent photographer and recorded many images at his workplace, a selection of which are featured here, as they are considered to be inextricably linked to the city's steam era.

Carlisle No. 5 signal box was situated at the south end of Citadel station and was probably the busiest box in the area having in excess of 100 levers, as pictured here. It would appear that signalman Wilf Scott (top) has been persuaded to make a rather striking pose for the camera, whilst Ken Runton (seated) and an unknown member of staff have both chosen more natural positions. The photographs, which have been taken just before midnight, if the wall clock is anything to go by, show two huge diagram boards which highlight the network of lines controlled from the box.

Nightshift with Dennis Smith in Carlisle No. 13 signal box which was located on the West Coast main line at Upperby Bridge Junction.

Left: **Drumburgh signal** box was on the Silloth branch and here we see the signalman there demonstrating the use of the electronic tablet system which was employed as a safe method of work for bi-directional traffic using a single line.

Right: **Another night-time** image which shows a signalman in Canal Junction box attending to the train describer unit which connected with the recently opened Kingmoor Power Signal Box (PSB) at the New Yard.

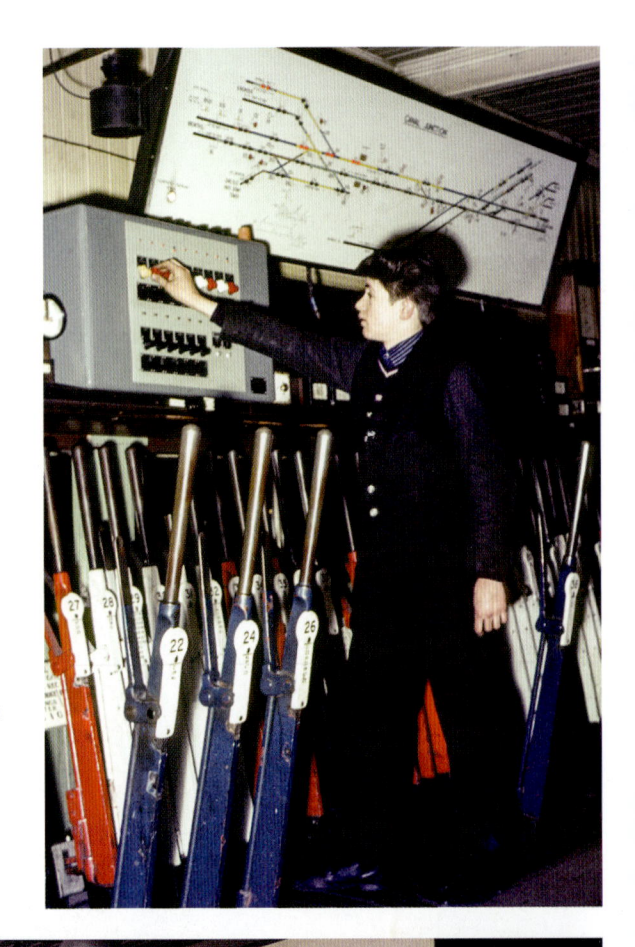

No.3 signal box was built by the Caledonian Railway and was situated on the West Coast main line near to Port Carlisle Branch Junction. Signalman A. McAmon wears the uniform so associated with railway staff during the 1950/1960 era. The diagram board shows that the lines that led into the Viaduct yard have been erased, an indication that dates the photograph to having been taken after the yard's closure in 1963.

Box No. 4A was merely a room that was located above platform 3 and it controlled all movements within Citadel station, as shown on the accompanying diagram.

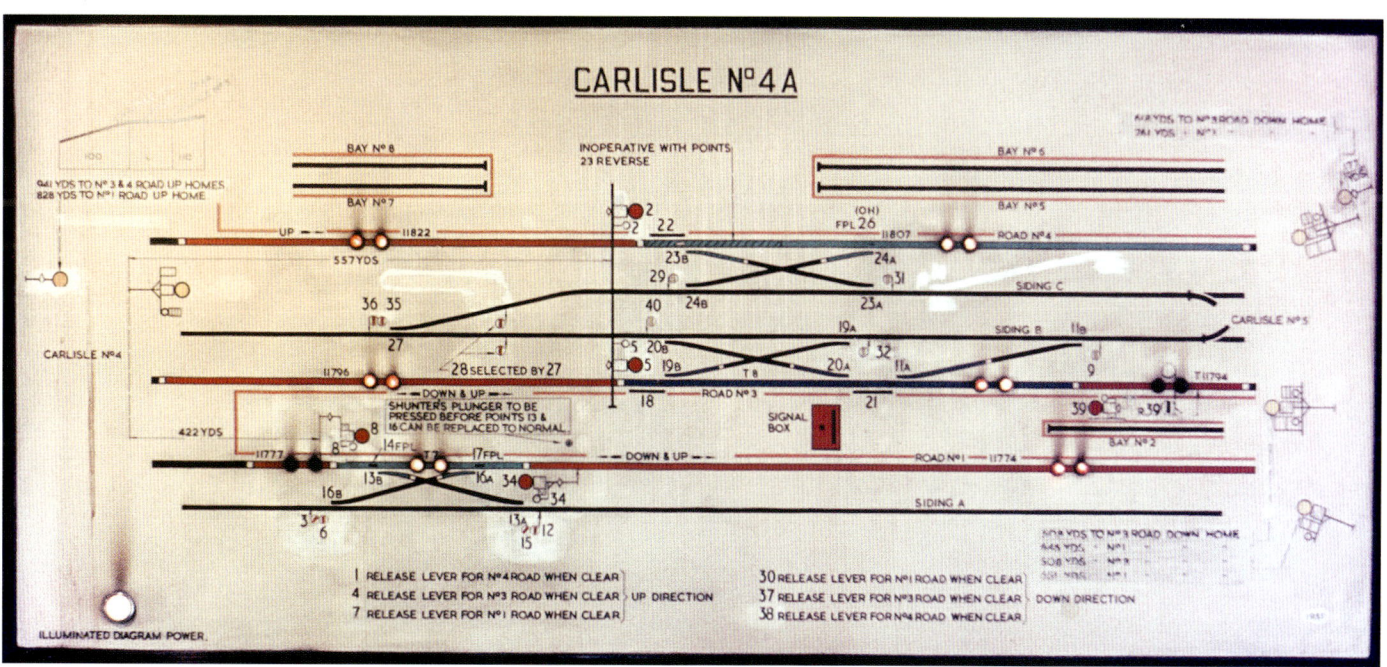

106 • THE LAST YEARS OF CARLISLE STEAM

Petteril Bridge
Junction signal box was situated where the Midland joined onto NER rails; London Road Junction (No. 7 box) is immediately beyond the overbridge seen in the distance. The diagram appears quite new and shows that the box is now also controlling the former NER lines to link with Corby Gates box.

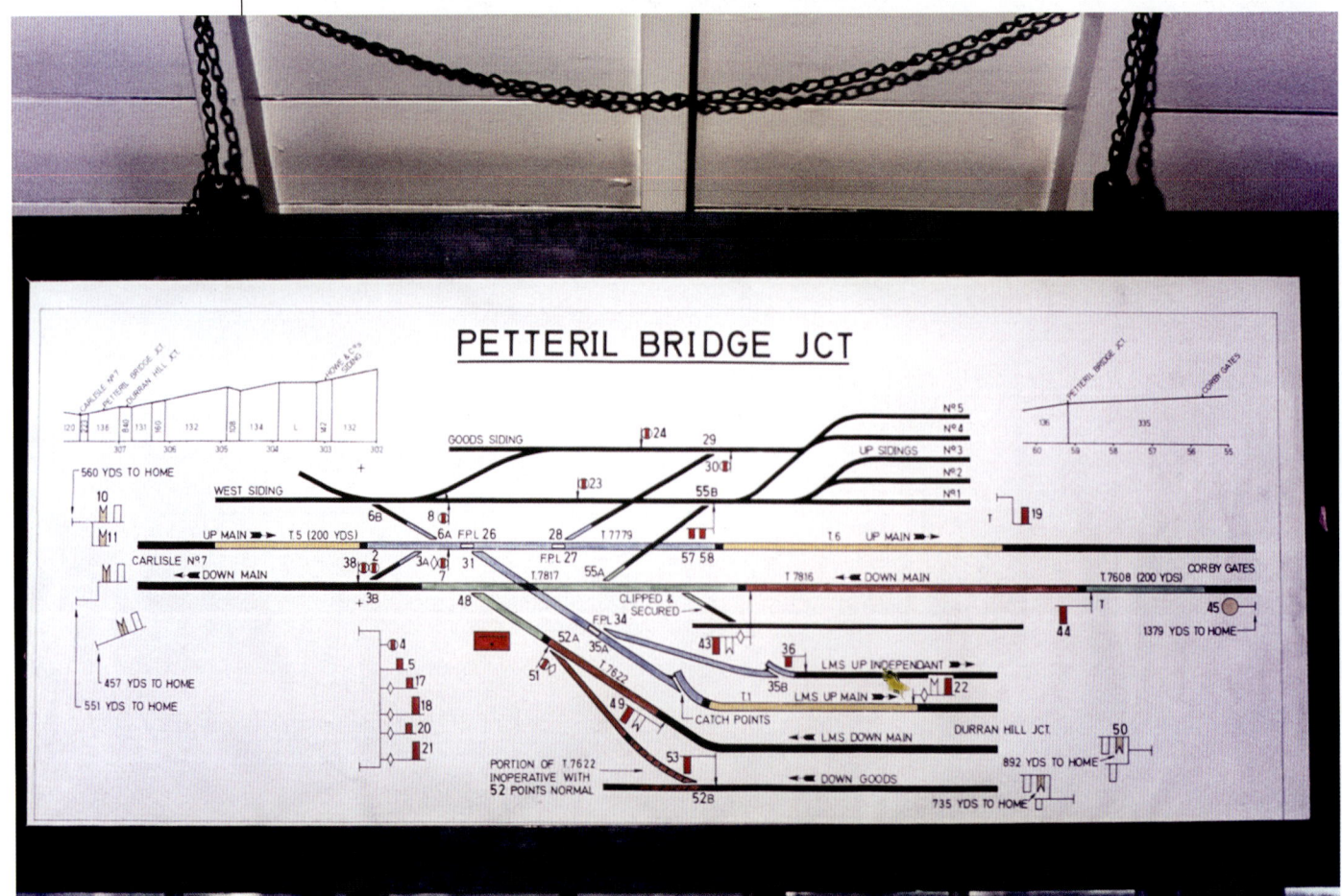

CHAPTER EIGHT
DEMISE IN COLOUR

Polmadie Princess Coronation 46222 *Queen Mary* has been turned and is ready to leave Kingmoor to back down to Citadel station in order to work the Royal Scot express to Glasgow Central. Although undated, there are a number of pointers which indicate that the photograph was taken no later than 1958; one of which is the lack of a speedometer, a device that was fitted to the class during 1957/58. *Colour Rail*

Another Pacific fully prepared to work a titled train, this time A3 60068 *Sir Visto*, waits on a signal at the mouth of the Canal shed prior to running down to the Citadel in order to work the down Waverley express in May 1959. Looking to be in an ex-works condition, the locomotive had been fitted with a double chimney during the previous month. *D.H. Beecroft/Colour Rail*

108 • THE LAST YEARS OF CARLISLE STEAM

Princess Royal Class 46203 *Princess Margaret Rose* is turned at Kingmoor on Saturday, 8 September 1962 before running tender first to Citadel station to relieve an incoming Euston to Perth express. This was to be the last northbound run for the locomotive, as upon its return to Kingmoor, 46203 was officially withdrawn from traffic. *Geoff Rixon*

There's grime, and then there is Kingmoor grime; the latter being suitably demonstrated by Stanier Jubilee 45629 *Straits Settlements* pictured at the 12A shed. Towards the end of the steam era, the cleaning of locomotives became less of a priority no doubt due to the dwindling numbers of staff previously employed for such a purpose. *Geoff Rixon*

DEMISE IN COLOUR • 109

Jubilee, 45738 *Samson*, receives final preparations prior to leaving Kingmoor during the early 1960s. *Geoff Rixon*

The BR Standard Class of Clan Pacifics totalled only ten in number and they were based equally between Kingmoor and Polmadie. The five at Kingmoor outlasted the Glasgow based ones by three years and one of the 12A allocation, 72009 *Clan Stewart*, is pictured at its home depot whilst in a gleaming ex-works condition. 72009 was transferred to 30A Stratford during 1958 in order for them to assess the capability of the locomotive before consideration was to be given for some members of the class to be transferred there. The locomotive was returned to Kingmoor within five weeks. When I asked Dick Hardy, who had been the Divisional Motive Power Superintendent at Stratford at that time, why that action was taken after such a short period, his reply was that they had it quickly returned because they didn't want to lose their allocation of Britannia Pacifics. *Geoff Rixon*

St Margaret's shed staff turned out an immaculate A3, 60052 *Prince Palatine,* for a Scottish Locomotive Preservation Fund rail tour on 4 June 1966 which ran from Edinburgh direct to Newcastle, then across to Carlisle, and back to Edinburgh via the Waverley route. Unfortunately, upon arrival at Carlisle, the locomotive was found to have developed a hot axle box and a call to Kingmoor to provide a replacement locomotive resulted in the appearance of a rather unkempt A4 60027 *Merlin* for the last leg of the tour. *Geoff Hamsher*

A locomotive that was destined to become the last one standing, this time from a class of 190 Jubilees, 45562 *Alberta* from Leeds Holbeck shed, takes on water at Kingmoor during 1967 no doubt after working north over the Settle-Carlisle line . *Ken Armstrong*

DEMISE IN COLOUR • 111

Britannia 70013 *Oliver Cromwell* was the last steam locomotive to receive an overhaul at Crewe Works and it was returned to Kingmoor in February 1967. Upon closure of the Carlisle shed, 70013 was transferred to Carnforth to be made available for hauling a number of special workings associated with the forthcoming end of steam. *Ken Armstrong*

There is quite a contrast in the external condition of the two locomotives on show at Kingmoor in 1967 between an ex works 70013, and a work stained Wigan Springs Branch based Black Five 45048. *Ken Armstrong*

112 • THE LAST YEARS OF CARLISLE STEAM

At this late stage of steam's existence at Kingmoor there probably was not much choice available to the shed staff to quickly ready an engine for breakdown crane duty. 70051 *Firth of Forth* is pictured with the Cowan & Sheldon built 75 ton crane on a date which appears close to the closure of the depot. *Derek Glover*

The changing scene at Etterby Junction features the old alongside the new. The Caledonian built their steam shed at Kingmoor in 1875 but it is soon to be replaced with the opening of the new diesel depot there. Former Great Western Castle Class 7029 *Clun Castle*, then privately owned, has been serviced at Kingmoor and is en route to Citadel station to work the return LCGB Castle to Carlisle rail tour over the S&C on 14 October 1967. *Ken Armstrong*

Enveloped in steam, Britannia 70013 *Oliver Cromwell* has the honour of heading the last ever steam hauled passenger train out of Carlisle with a football special en route to Blackpool on Boxing Day, 1967. The two photographs have been taken from both sides of St Nicholas Bridge, and show the special train climbing away from Citadel station and then its progression towards Upperby, a scene enhanced by a weak and wintry sun. Upon 70013's arrival back at Carlisle, the curtain was brought down on steam hauled passenger workings, it then only left 70045 *Lord Rowallan* to work the final goods train out of the city four days later, and that was the end of everyday steam in Carlisle. *C. Blezard (both)*

114 • THE LAST YEARS OF CARLISLE STEAM

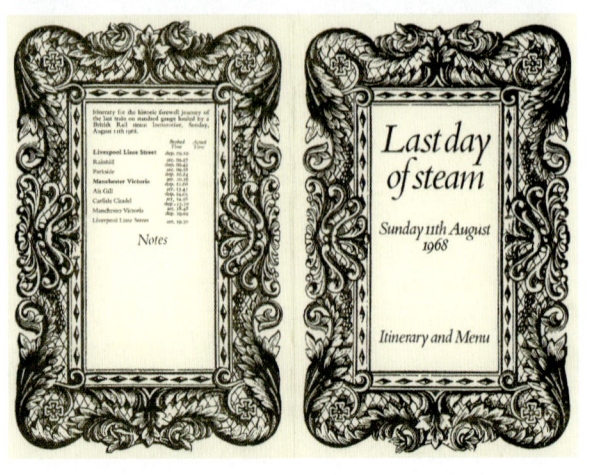

CHAPTER NINE
1T57

***Above, below and opposite*: On 11** August 1968, British Railways ran its final steam hauled train, the infamous 1T57, also known as the Fifteen Guinea Special, from Liverpool to Carlisle and return. Britannia 70013 *Oliver Cromwell* worked the leg from Manchester Victoria via Blackburn and Settle to Carlisle and is pictured at Ais Gill where it had paused for nothing more than a photo stop. Once at Carlisle, 70013 was detached whilst a double-headed combination of two Black Five locomotives, 44871 and 44781, coupled to the other end of the stock before returning the commemorative train back to Manchester. *Oliver Cromwell* followed a short time later down the former Midland line and once that occurred, that was really it; Carlisle had become a steam free zone. *Peter Fitton (all three)*

BIBLIOGRAPHY

BOOKS
Rail Centres: Carlisle by Peter W. Robinson, Ian Allan, 1986
The Settle and Carlisle Railway by O.S. Nock, Patrick Stephens Limited, 1992
LMS Jubilees by R.J. Essery and G. Toms, Wild Swan Publications, 1994
Locomotives of the LNER Part 2A by RCTS, 1997
6233 Duchess of Sutherland and the Princess Coronation Class by Brell Ewart & Brian Radford, Princess Royal Class Locomotive Trust, 2002

WEBSITES
Six Bells Junction
BR Database, incorporating the input by the Stephenson Locomotive Society (SLS)